New South Wales in Australia abounds with beautiful birds!

Birdlife International lists 722 different species in Australia – 832 if we include vagrants and introduced species. New South Wales reportedly contains close to 600 of these.

We would like to invite you to embark on a captivating journey through the diverse and enchanting world of more than 150 of the most common bird species that call this region home.

This coffee table book is more than a collection of photographs; it is a celebration of the diversity and beauty of nature in this part of the world. In addition to the photographs, we have added some facts and comments which you will hopefully find interesting- even a few poems.

Happy birding!

Dirk Kotze and Sue O'Connell

How to navigate:
There is an index of birds at the end. Some photographs are grouped by type of birds (like Honeyeaters), others by where they were seen. Names on pages are ordered top left, top right, bottom left, etc.

Parrots

Decked out
like carnival queens
Gaudy, lurid, ostentatious
Swaggering, strutting
Owning the forest
X-factor birds

Page 1 - Australian Grebe at Tuggerah

This page - Galah at Lane Cove National Park

Male and female Australian King-Parrots in Lane Cove National Park, scouting tree hollows for a nest. Parrots are prime examples of the dazzling array of colours that birds have developed through evolution. Yet, birds can see even more colours than what we can observe in their plumage. This is thanks to additional colour cones in their retinas that are sensitive to the ultraviolet range. King-Parrots appear distinctly red and green to us, but under ultraviolet light, their wing feathers also show a prominent yellow glow. (1)

Little Corellas are playful birds. They sometimes slide down the steep roofs of wheat silos, falling off the edge and then flying back to the top to slide down again. They have also been seen perched on the blades of windmills - spinning round and around, falling off and then regaining a precarious grip on the blades. Even when they are perched, they often hang upside down, or dangle below the perch, holding on with their bills. When they play, they become very noisy. They have conversations with one another, fly around and show off. (2) This fun-loving trio was hanging out at Centennial Park.

Rainbow Lorikeets (birds of a feather) at Lane Cove National Park - near Kissing Point.

Superb Parrots are listed as vulnerable in the Australian Environment Protection and Biodiversity Conservation Act 1999. The total population is estimated to be only a few thousand birds.

In 2008 the NPWS pleaded with truck drivers to cover their trucks properly after reports that more than 20 endangered Superb Parrots died near Canberra after eating too much spilled grain.

A spokesman said: "*It's very attractive to them and they sit there eating it, unaware that a car is coming along at 110km/h. They just stuff themselves with the grain ... but the more they eat the slower they become. A car comes along, and their natural instincts don't serve them well, and they end up on the grille of the car.*" (3)

Eastern Rosella at the Wianamatta Regional Park in Ropes Crossing

Opposite: Crimson Rosella in Lane Cove National Park.
These birds are not only colourful, but they are also smelly. They have been described as "smelling like an old jumper, which has been drenched in really cheap perfume". The scent is thought to help the birds communicate and regulate nesting behaviour – for example if a female can smell that a male of the same species has been around, she will arrive back to the nest quicker and stay for longer. On the downside, the smell of the birds helps ringtail possums (preying on the eggs) to locate their nests. (4)

Red-rumped Parrot.
The red rump mainly shows when in flight and is only present on the male. Otherwise, the overall impression is yellow, green, turquoise, and blue. Females are more brownish dull.

Gang-Gang Cockatoos at Barren Grounds Nature Reserve. The male sports a scarlet red head and a wispy crest. These birds have an unmistakable call – described as the sound of a squeaky gate or a cork being pulled from a bottle.

Yellow-tailed Black-Cockatoo at Ramsgate

Glossy Black-Cockatoo on the Narabeen Lagoon trail

Sulphur-crested Cockatoo

These birds are the masters of the loud, raucous, unpleasant screech. Some say they pack more decibels than a jet engine, but that may depend on your distance from the engine!

A few years ago, a depiction of a yellow-crested Cockatoo was found in a falconry book owned by Holy Roman Emperor Frederick II. Dated c 1250 it predates other European depictions of cockatoos by c 250 years. The birds are only found in Australia, Papua New Guinea, and islands off the Indonesian sea. The discovery may change the current understanding of historic European trade links with this part of the world. (5)

Agora

Sydney-siders scurry

into shiny tower blocks

"cabined, cribbed, confined"

No time to dream

While parkland, bushland teem

A cacophonous chorus calls

I stretch my legs

Australian White Ibis (a.k.a. Bin Chicken!) in Hyde Park

Australian Brush-Turkey at Bradleys Head.

Researchers from the University of Montana believe brush turkeys could be living models of how dinosaurs evolved into birds.

To test the theory, they lugged adjustable ramps into a field, caught brush turkeys of various ages and filmed them as they tried to run up the ramps.

Surprisingly, they found that infants outperformed their parents. Hatchlings used their wings to a greater extent while the older birds relied on their big strong legs, mostly ignoring the wings.

Some types of proto-bird dinosaurs with small wing-like structures apparently changed their plumage as they got older, suggesting that feathers and wings might have served a variety of purposes, depending on the age of the creature. (6)

Dusky Moorhen and Purple Swamphen – both at Centennial Park

In June 2017 at least 10 people were treated by a local optometrist after being attacked by a single bird at Kiama Village shopping centre. The council attempted to deter the bird which was believed to be a native "Pee Wee" (Magpie Lark) from swooping shoppers, with the installation of two imitation owls. (7) This Pee Wee was seen at Botany Bay.

Sparrow at Dee Why and Pied Butcherbird in the Capertee Valley

In a 2017 poll run by The Guardian, the Australian Magpie was voted as the country's bird of the year, narrowly beating the White Ibis.

The bird's popularity is likely due to its great vocal range as well as its ability to recognise faces and hence form bonds with people. (8)

Welcome Swallow at Narabeen.
Australian Wood Duck with chicks at the Sydney Botanic Garden

Opposite: Pied Currawong at Centennial Park

Opposite: Hardhead, Eurasian Coot and Pacific Black Duck stretching its wings. All at Centennial Park.

Above: Pair of Red-necked Avocets at Badu Mangroves, Olympic Park. Scientists have reported that birds with bigger beaks spend more time covering their beaks under their wings to prevent heat loss. Birds with bigger beaks get cold noses! These upturned proboscises would therefore be really chilled on a winter's day. Birds who cover their beaks under their wings cannot be very good at looking out for predators. It has been found that Avocets cover their beaks more often when they are in bigger flocks with more birds to keep a look-out. (9)

Female and male Chestnut Teals at Warriewood Wetlands.

They form monogamous pairs that stay together outside the breeding season, defend the nest site, and look after the young when hatched.

These birds are omnivorous. While they, by far, prefer plant materials, they will also eat small animals. They have been observed following pelicans and devouring the pond life disturbed by the larger birds. (10)

Like other swans, the Black Swan is largely monogamous, pairing for life. Albatrosses are the only birds considered to have a zero divorce rate. In Black Swans, the break-up rate is about 6%. They are, however, regularly unfaithful – around 1 in 7 eggs reared by a Black Swan male will not be his, usually because the female has copulated with a different male, just in case she cannot have offspring with her partner.

An estimated quarter of all pairings are homosexual, mostly between males. Homosexual males may temporarily associate with a female mate and then break up the bond once the eggs have been laid. Otherwise, they may usurp nests or steal eggs from male/female clutches. These male pairs perform parenting duties, including incubation, and caring for cygnets. (11)

Pink-eared Ducks – named after an insignificant patch of pink feathers on the side of their heads. Some call them Zebra Ducks – for more obvious reasons. They feed by sucking in water through the tip of their bills and then filtering it out the side.

Common Mynah at the Royal Botanic Garden

Noisy Miners at Royal Botanic Garden. Despite their similar sounding names, they are not related to the Common Mynah. The Noisy Miner is an Australian Honeyeater while the Common Mynah, introduced from South-East Asia, is a scavenger related to starlings. An internet search delivers several options for buying or building traps to control the Common Mynah, referred to as "rats of the sky" which "have become a major threat to our native bird life".

However, a 2014 study showed that Noisy Miners are the bigger threat to native bird life diversity. They actively exclude all other birds from their territories in urban landscapes and remnant woodlands. They thrive in these habitats dominated by trees and grass. Yet, studies have not detected major impacts on native birds from the Mynah, which prefers to nest in roofs. There is little evidence that it is moving into "natural" habitats. The study found that the cull of Noisy Miners could dramatically increase the number and variety of birds. (12)

Pelagic Birds of the Pacific

Tiny boat rocks from side to side
White knuckles – scanning the horizon
Photographers don't come with sea legs
Shearwaters skim the surface
"Providence Petrel over here!"
Pomarine Jaeger tails into the wind
Flash of white – Gannet – it's gone
Fool!
Track, focus, shoot, again
Tumult
Distilled to an image

Previous: Pomarine Jaeger. "Pomarine" from Greek, meaning lid-nose. The bill is ridged because the nostrils are roofed by a horned plate.

Osprey at Long Reef Collaroy.

Wedge-tailed- and Flesh Footed Shearwaters. Shearwaters spend most of their lives on the open ocean, approaching land only long enough to breed. They have specially adapted eyesight to spot and accurately grab fish below the surface (13)

Australasian Gannet fishing at Balmoral Beach. In the dive, they can reach up to 100km/h

Opposite: Crested Tern, Little Tern, Silver Gull, Kelp Gull.
This page: Pacific Gull – Australia's largest gull

Top left: Little Black Cormorants at The Spit

Pied Cormorant (left) and Little Pied Cormorant (top right) at Olympic Park

Opposite: Great Cormorant on Sydney harbour

Opposite - Darter at Barangaroo

This page: A pod of Australian Pelicans at The Entrance. There are seven species of pelicans in the world. The Australian Pelican is medium-sized by pelican standards with a wingspan of 2,3-2,6m. However, the pale, pinkish bill is enormous and is the largest bill of any bird in the world. (14)

Sydney Olympic Park
On a fine day
You can catch the ferry to
Olympic Park
Cheaper on a Sunday
The birds are sweet
And the cyclists
Politely ring their bells

Brown Quail at Wentworth Common.

The Brown Quail is one of the species of birds which can be legally hunted under the New South Wales Native Bird Management Program.

Quail eggs are popular as a novelty food in many parts of the world. The eggs have a higher yolk ratio than chicken eggs and contain a higher proportion of vitamin A. (15)

Black-winged Stilts at Badhu Mangroves. Their nests may be anything from a simple shallow scrape on the ground to a mound of vegetation placed on or near the water. Both sexes incubate the eggs and look after the young.

Opposite: Laughing Kookaburra

This page: Grey Butcherbird, Forest Kingfisher – both at the Badhu Mangroves.

The kookaburra is a species of kingfisher, but the butcherbird is not related to the kingfishers. The Grey Butcherbird may not seem particularly intimidating, but it is an aggressive predator, hunting small animals, birds and insects. Uneaten food may be stored in a tree fork or impaled on a branch.(16)

Little Pied Cormorant (left) and Pied Cormorant at Shipwreck Lookout. Useful pose to spot the differences between the two species.

Opposite: Striated Heron (also known as Mangrove Heron) also at Shipwreck Lookout. "Striated" because it is striped and not often spotted!
These birds are quite shy and spend much of their time skulking next to the riverbank looking for fish or small animals. Sometimes they may attract fish by dropping a leaf into the water to get their attention.

Red-browed Finch near the bird hide.

Sacred Kingfisher at Badhu Mangroves,
Rufous Whistler on the Chiltern Trail in Ku-ring-gai Chase National Park
Golden-headed Cisticola (pronounced "sis-tick-ler"). This bird skilfully sews leaves together with cobweb to make a nest. This has earned it the alternative common name of Tailorbird. (17)

Opposite: Nankeen Kestrel taking a break on a very windy day at Long Reef.

This page: Black-shouldered Kite with catch. Black-shouldered Kites have become specialist predators on the introduced house mouse, often following outbreaks of mouse plagues in rural areas.

Opposite: Powerful Owls – mother and chick. The largest owl in Australia – up to 60 cm with a wingspan up to 1.4m. These two were spotted in a fig tree in Centennial Park

This page: Tawny Frogmouth. They hunt at night and hide during the day. However, they are not owls. Owls have strong legs and powerful talons to get their prey while frogmouths catch their prey with their beak and have fairly weak feet. Tawny Frogmouths have wide, forward facing beaks to catch insects whereas owls have narrow downward facing beaks to tear the prey apart. (18)

White-faced Heron "leaving no stone unturned" at Long Reef Collaroy.

Intermediate Egret at the Badhu Mangroves

Straw-necked Ibis showing off its throat plumes.

Masked Lapwing with a sandworm at The Spit

Opposite: Female and male Variegated Fairy-wrens at Tuggerah
This page: Immature and mature male Superb Fairywrens at Badhu Mangroves

Australasian wrens are not related to true wrens, but are more closely related to Honeyeaters and Pardalotes. Their similarity to wrens of North America & Europe could simply be the consequence of convergent evolution between unrelated species that share the same ecological niche. (19)

Central Coast

Tuggerah Terrigal The Entrance
Bowerbid Bellbird Dollarbird
Parakeet Pelican Pardelote
Rose Robin Flame Robin Yellow Robin
Flycatcher Fantail Fairy-wren
Magic places Magic Birds

The Rose Robin on this page and most of the birds on the following pages were spotted in the vicinity the Macpherson's Road Swamp or the Tuggerah Sewage Treatment Works where the nutrient-rich water attracts a variety of birds to the lake and the surrounding bush.

Tuggerah Lakes and the forests around them have been designated by Birdlife International as an Important Bird Area (IBA). IBA's are areas of the world that are globally important to at least one species of bird.

Opposite: Striated Thornbill, Brown Thornbill, Yellow Thornbill, Varied Sittella

This page: Leaden Flycatcher, Mistletoebird (also known as the Mistletoe Flowerpecker) and White-throated Treecreeper

Eastern Yellow Robin

Black-faced Cuckoo Shrike

White-browed Scrubwren

Chestnut-breasted Mannikin

Brown Gerygone
(Rhymes with Antegone. Pretty bird i'n he?)

Gerygone is a Greek word that can be translated as "born of sound" – after their melodious songs

Flame Robin

Eastern Whipbird near the boardwalk – Long Reef Collaroy

Opposite: Bell Miner (or Bellbird) in the forest near Kissingpoint Road. There is a large number of Bellbirds in this area (the sounds are unmistakable) and there are concerns that they may be driving more rare species from their habitat.

Common Starling

Silvereye

Grey Fantail

Restless Flycatcher

Tree Martin with hungry chicks

Golden Whistler

The Dollarbird is the only Roller to be found in Australia. Rollers are so named because of their rolling courtship flight displays. "Dollar" refers to the prominent white patches (resembling silver dollars) displayed on each wing when the bird is in flight. (20)

Olive-backed Oriole

Figbird. Two Figbird races occur in Australia - the Yellow Figbird in northeastern parts and the southern race (on the far right) known as the "Green Figbird". This one was seen in Kiama. (21)

White-necked Heron. Non-breeding plumage on the left and breeding plumage (all white neck) on the right.

Bailon's Crake hunting in the "nutrient rich" water of Tuggerah Sewage Works

Grey Shrike-thrush.

Fan-tailed Cuckoo at Barren Grounds Nature Reserve, enjoying its favourite meal - a hairy caterpillar.

White-winged Chough. The nest of the White-winged Chough is a large bowl of mud, which is built on a horizontal branch. It may take several months to build if there is insufficient rain to moisten the mud. If there is a lack of mud, birds may use cattle or emu dung. (22)

Red-whiskered Bulbul at Spring Creek, Kiama

Down from the high tree tops you float
Colourful little Pardalote
To build your nest upon the ground
A leafy, twiggy hidden mound
Flitting back and forth no rest
Tiny eggs snug in your nest
Fleetingly adorn the land before
Up to the Eucalypt canopy you soar

Female and male Spotted Pardalotes off Chiltern Road, Ku-ring-gai Chase National Park. Pardelotes can normally be found in the upper branches of tall trees, but they nest close to the ground. In this relatively short window one has a chance to see them from closer up.

Wee Willy Wagtail

Wee Willy Wagtail flies round the land

Right-wag and left-wag, plumage oh so grand

Darting at the insects, catching those in flight

Pretty little fantail

Got it in one bite

A bevy of doves!

Brown Cuckoo-Dove at Lane Cove National Park.

Opposite:
Crested Pigeon at Ramsgate
Spotted Turtle-Dove at Curl Curl
Bar-shouldered Dove in Ku-ring-gai Chase
Peaceful Dove in the Capertee Valley

Capertee Valley Haiku

Capertee beckons
Rich with a promise of birds
Suspense in the air

Brown Falcon taking off

White-bellied Sea-Eagle. In 1949, Malay cinema magnate, ornithologist and philanthropist, Loke Wan Tho had a 40-meter high (about 13 storey) tower built for the sole purpose of observing a White-bellied Sea-Eagle nest in the palace gardens of Istana Bukit Serene in Johor Bahru. On weekends he spent hours perched in the shaky tower, taking photographs and waiting for the egg to hatch. Unfortunately, the egg turned out to be addled, but the pictures he took were published in *The Illustrated London News in 1954*. (23)

Australian Hobby

Whistling Kite

Opposite: Southern Whiteface, Diamond Fire-tail, Double-barred Finch, Crested Shrike-tit

This page: Jackie Winter

The Capertee Valley is recognised internationally as an Important Bird Area and one of the top 50 bird watching places in the world. The diverse habitat provides home to an abundance of bird species - approximately 242 recorded.

The valley is a transition zone between the forest of the Blue Mountains and woodlands, farm- and grasslands. Here you can find grassland finches, reasonably close to Sydney. (24)

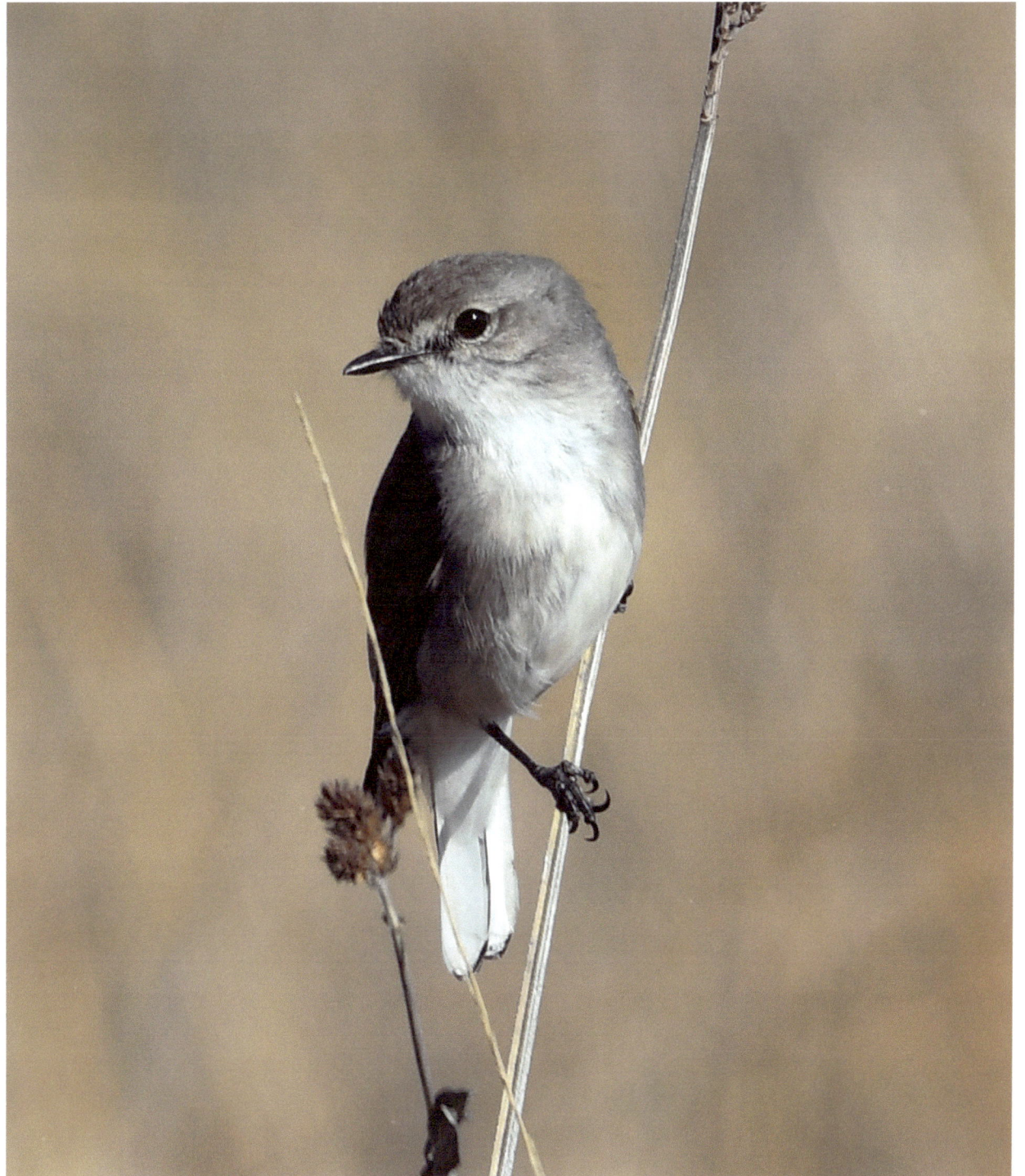

HONEYEATERS OF KU-RING-GAI CHASE

Sunbirds of the South
What an array
of colour and design!
A flash of plumage
recedes behind a leaf
Sirens of the forest
You enthral and enchant
With your fine curved bill
Your brush-tipped tongue
You beautify the bush

New Holland Honeyeater - brush-tipped tongue on full display. With long slender beaks and a tongue which can protrude well beyond their beaks, they are able to probe for nectar in the deep flowers of Banksias and Grevilleas.

Lewin's Honeyeater - one of two birds named after John Lewin – an English-born artist active in Australia from 1800. He was the first professional artist of the colony of New South Wales and illustrated the earliest volumes of Australian natural history. Only six copies of his book *Birds of New Holland with their Natural History* have survived. An 1813 edition with the amended title *Birds of New South Wales* was the first illustrated book to be engraved and printed in Australia. Only 13 copies are still in existence, and it is regarded as one of the great Australian bibliographic rarities. (25)

White-plumed Honeyeater

Opposite: White-eared Honeyeater, White-cheeked Honeyeater, Eastern Spinebill and Scarlet Honeyeater (earlier colonial name was "Little Soldier Bird" because it may look like it is wearing a red coat).

Yellow-tufted Honeyeater, Noisy Friarbird

Opposite: White-naped Honeyeater, Yellow-faced Honeyeater

Near the end of the Chiltern Road, a dead-end narrow road in Ingelside, leading to the edge of Ku-ring-gai Chase, is a dusty trail – more of a fire break than an actual trail, only about 2 kilometres in length.

This dusty anonymous path that seems to hold little promise, is a fantastic place to see honeyeaters. Within a few hundred metres from the start of the trail we have sometimes seen as many as many as four or five different species.

Opposite: Litte Wattlebird, Red Wattlebird

Satin Bowerbird (female) at Blue Mountains Botanic Garden, near Mount Tomah

Regent Bowerbird, near MacPherson's swamp, Tuggerah.
All male Bowerbirds build bowers, from simple ground clearings to elaborate structures, to attract females. Regent Bowerbirds mix a muddy grey-ish blue or pea green "saliva paint" in their mouths, which they use to decorate their bowers. The male builds an avenue-type bower consisting of two walls of sticks, decorated with shells, seeds, leaves and berries. Regents will sometimes use wads of greenish leaves as "paintbrushes" to help spread the "paint", representing one of the few known instances of tools used by birds. (26).

Waders

Graceful foragers of the shoreline

Opposite:
Pied Oystercatcher at The Entrance, Sooty Oystercatcher at Huskisson Beach, Jervis Bay

Red-kneed Dotterel and Black-fronted Dotterel - both at Pitt Town Lagoon

Ruddy Turnstone doing what he does best

Pacific Golden Plover

All at Long Reef, Collaroy:

Grey-tailed Tattler

Red-necked Stint

Double-banded Plover

Bar-tailed Godwit

Black-tailed Godwit

Sharp-tailed Sandpipers

Well camouflaged Latham's Snipe

Little Egret in breeding plumage

Royal Spoonbill at Centennial Park, sporting its finest breeding plumes. In fairly shallow water, Royal Spoonbills use several methods to catch food; slow sweeping from side to side with an open bill, rapid sweeping while walking fast or even running through the water, as well as dragging, probing or grabbing.

The spatulate bill has many vibration detectors, called papillae, on the inside of the spoon, which means the bird can feel for prey even in murky water and can feed by day and night. (27)

Cattle Egret looking sheepish on a farm near Tuggerah.

Yellow Spoonbill in the Capertee Valley - less glamorous but slightly bigger cousin of the Royal Spoonbill.

Opposite: Great Egret in breeding plumage.

Opposite: White-faced Heron fishing. Like other long necked herons, it fishes using a bill stab while the rest of the body can remain motionless. This is made possible by its elongated six cervical vertebra acting as a hinge.

Three Silver Gulls at Huskisson Beach, Jervis Bay.

Superb Lyrebird in the Minnamurra Rainforest - Budderoo National Park.

Bush Stone-curlew

Overleaf: The word Emu supposedly comes from the 17th C Portuguese 'ema', meaning large bird. The birds can be found in the wild in New South Wales - some even in Ropes Crossing in the Greater Western Sydney region. The pigeon here obligingly positioned itself to enable size comparison.

References

1. Australian Museum. Australian King-Parrot. Retrieved November 2018 from https://australianmuseum.net.au/australian-king-parrot
2. Birdlife Australia. Little Corella. Retrieved November 2018 from http://birdlife.org.au/bird-profile/little-corella
3. ABC News. Endangered superb parrots dying in 'catastrophic' strikes on NSW road. Retrieved November 2018 from https://www.abc.net.au/news/2018-01-12/superb-parrots-dying-in-road-strikes-in-nsw/9322938
4. Phys. Org. Feathers have their own scents, and predators know it. Retrieved November 2018 from https://phys.org/news/2017-11-feathers-scents-predators.html
5. BBC News. Cockatoo identified in 13th century European book. Retrieved September 2018 from https://www.bbc.com/news/world-australia-44610271
6. LiveScience. Turkey Runs Like Winged Dinosaurs, Scientists Think (2018). Retrieved June 2018 from https://www.livescience.com/10216-turkey-runs-winged-dinosaurs-scientists.html
7. Illawarra Mercury. 'Pecked in the eye': menacing bird attacking shoppers in Kiama. Retrieved September 2018 from https://www.illawarramercury.com.au/story/4735116/pecked-in-the-eye-menacing-bird-attacking-shopper-in-kiama/
8. The Guardian. Australian Magpie wins bird of the year poll. Retrieved November 2018 from https://www.theguardian.com/environment/live/2017/dec/11/bird-of-the-year-150000-votes-counted-as-ibis-fans-anxiously-await-results
9. Popular Science. Birds with bigger beaks get colder noses. Retrieved September 2018 from https://www.aol.com/article/news/2017/01/05/birds-with-bigger-beaks-get-colder-noses/21648394
10. Goulburn Wetlands: Chestnut Teal. Retrieved June 2018 from http://goulburnwetlands.org.au/?pageid=510
11. Oxford Academic: Behavioural Ecology (2006). Same-sex sexual behaviour in birds. Retrieved June 2018 from https://academic.oup.com/beheco/article/18/1/21/209396
12. ABC News. Native Noisy Miners cause more damage than introduced Indian Mynah, research finds (December 2014). Retrieved June 2018 from http://www.abc.net.au/news/2014-12-14/native-noisy-miners-cause-more-damage-than-introduced-species/5964328
13. Journal of experimental Biology. Microspectrophotometry of visual pigments and oil droplets in a marine bird (2004)/ Retrieved June 2018 from http://jeb.biologists.org/content/207/7/1229
14. Guinness World Records (2018). Longest bills. Retrieved November 2018 from http://www.guinnessworldrecords.com/world-records/longest-bills
15. NSW Department of Primary Industries. Hunting Game Birds in NSW. Retrieved November 2018 from https://www.dpi.nsw.gov.au/hunting/game-and-pests/native-game-birds
16. Birds in Backyards. Grey Butcherbird. Retrieved August 2018 from http://www.birdsinbackyards.net/species/Cracticus-torquatus
17. Birds in Backyards. Golden-headed Cisticola. Retrieved August 2018 from http://www.birdsinbackyards.net/species/Cisticola-exilis
18. Wikipedia. Tawny Frogmouth. Retrieved November 2018 from https://en.wikipedia.org/wiki/Tawny-frogmouth
19. Wikipedia. Australasian Wren. Retrieved November 2018 from https://en.wikipedia.org/wiki/Australasian-wren
20. Birds in Backyards. Dollarbird. Retrieved November 2018 from http://www.birdsinbackyards.net/species/Eurystomus-orientalis
21. Morcombe, M. Field Guide to Australian Birds (2003) p306
22. Birds in Backyards. White-winged Chough. Retrieved October 2018 from http://www.birdsinbackyards.net/species/Corcorax-melanorhamphos
23. Sanger, C Malcolm Macdonald: Bringing an end to empire (1995) p317. McGill-Queen's University Press: USA
24. Visitnsw.com. Capertee Valley bird trail. Retrieved November 2018 from https://www.visitnsw.com/destinations/blue-mountains/lithgow-area/lithgow/attractions/capertee-valley-bird-trail
25. Wikipedia. John Lewin. Retrieved November 2018 from https://en.wikipedia.org/wiki/John-Lewin
26. Beauty of Birds. Regent Bowerbird. Retrieved October 2018 from https://www.beautyofbirds.com/regentbowerbirds.html
27. Australian Museum. Royal Spoonbill. Retrieved September 2018 from https://australianmuseum.net.au/royal-spoonbill-platalae-regia

INDEX

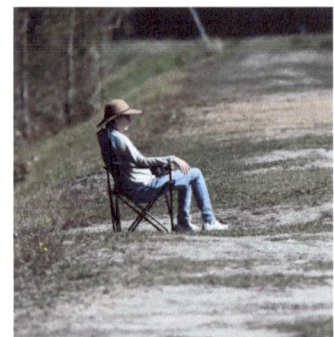

Left: Wedge-tailed Eagle
Swift Parrot
Fuscous Honeyeater

Right: Shining Bronze Cuckoo
Brown Treecreeper
Twitcher

www.ingramcontent.com/pod-product-compliance
Lightning Source LLC
Chambersburg PA
CBHW041225020426

42333CB00004B/60